THE
POWER
OF
DEVOTED
PRAYER

MIKE NOVOTNY AND MARK JESKE

Published by Straight Talk Books
P.O. Box 301, Milwaukee, WI 53201
800.661.3311 • timeofgrace.org

Scripture is taken from THE HOLY BIBLE, NEW INTERNATIONAL VERSION®, NIV®. Copyright © 1973, 1978, 1984, 2011 by Biblica, Inc.® Used by permission. All rights reserved worldwide.

Printed in the United States of America
ISBN: 978-1-949488-47-0

Ask and it will be given to you; seek and you will find; knock and the door will be opened to you.

Matthew 7:7

INTRODUCTION

Okay, confession time. I stink at prayer. *Stink* might be a strong verb, but it's the right one. I've tried prayer apps, repeating calendar reminders, journaling, and a dozen other systems over the years, but prayer feels way harder than reading my Bible or going to church. You too? Recently, I started keeping track of my blocks of dedicated, personal prayer time. After two months, I tallied up all the minutes and ended up with . . . 15. Not 15 *hours* of prayer, but 15 *minutes*. In 2 months. Yikes.

But I'm not giving up. I'm re-devoting myself to the kind of prayer the apostles embraced. **"They devoted themselves . . . to prayer"** (Acts 2:42). Why try prayer again? Because prayer works. The devil fears people who persist in prayer. And I've seen the power of prayer among my church family. When a small group of Christians starts a texting thread that is always open for prayer, God does amazing stuff in their hearts and at their church. When we pray the gospel over each other, God does amazing stuff, breaking chains of guilt and erasing years of shame. When we don't see prayer as the token starter pistol for dinner or the closing requirement before bed but as a privilege and a power source, God does amazing stuff. So even if the new habit is hard, prayer is worth it. God is listening. And he can't wait to hear the sound of your voice.

Would you join me in prayer today? Would you join me in devoting yourself to using this journal to learn more about prayer and to take more time for it? God would love to hear from you more!

PRAYER OBSTACLES

Pastor Mark Jeske

ARROGANCE

**"What shall I do? I have no place to store my crops."
Then he said, "This is what I'll do. I will tear down my barns
and build bigger ones, and there I will store all
my surplus grain. And I'll say to myself, 'You have plenty of
grain laid up for many years. Take life easy; eat, drink and be
merry.'" But God said to him, "You fool!"**

Luke 12:17-20

Is it good to be self-reliant? Of course. If you are a parent, you have spent years and huge amounts of energy teaching and training your kids to take care of themselves. Self-reliance is good. Self-absorption is not.

I know one reason why people don't pray much and why God doesn't hear from me more: arrogance. When you're pretty full of yourself and think you can do it all, praying seems like begging, or worse, a waste of time.

Jesus told a story about a farmer who thought his huge profits were realized because he was such a genius: "'What shall I do? I have no place to store my crops.' Then he said, 'This is what I'll do. I will tear down my barns and build bigger ones, and there I will store all my surplus grain. And I'll say to myself, "You have plenty of grain laid up for many years. Take life easy; eat, drink and be merry."' But God said to him, 'You fool!'" (Luke 12:17-20).

I think that's one major reason why God lets people, including his believers, suffer. It is vital that we see our limitations, our sin, our mortality. We utterly depend on God's providing and forgiveness every day.

Practice with me: "Lord, I need you. Help me today."

Journaling Question

Describe a challenging time in your life when you really leaned on God to get you through each day. After it was over, did you feel that your faith/prayer life grew stronger as a result? Why do you think that was?

Prayer

Dear heavenly Father, help me remember that I need you during the good times of my life as well as the bad. Help me rely on you every day and call out to you in every season. Amen.

GUILT

**Come to me, all you who are weary and
burdened, and I will give you rest.**

Matthew 11:28

When I was a kid, we always knew that when the dog slunk around the house and avoided our eyes, we would soon find an "accident." When you know that you have done wrong and offended someone, it is a powerful deterrent to wanting to have an intimate conversation with that person. Guilt makes you want to run away. An ashamed first couple hid in the bushes when they heard God's "footsteps" in the garden. When we are guilty of unconfessed and unforgiven sin, one of the first casualties is our desire to pray.

Here is the beauty of a relationship with our God that is based not on *our* performance and behavior but rather on *his* grace, that is, his decision to love and forgive us unconditionally. Jesus came to this earth to rescue sinful and ashamed fools like you and me. He said, "Come to me, all you who are weary and burdened, and I will give you rest" (Matthew 11:28).

When you are aware of your shortcomings, your conscience makes you sick inside, and you are too ashamed to pray, that is the very best time to pray and claim the forgiveness that was bought for you. God's mercy is bigger than your sin. He will never despise a broken and contrite heart (Psalm 51:17); in fact, his particular specialty is in healing broken hearts and providing rest for restless spirits.

Journaling Question

Is there anything preventing you from coming to God in prayer? Make a list of your fears and concerns, as well as anything you might be feeling ashamed of. Now draw a thin line through each item (so you can still read what you wrote), and at the top of the list, write: GRACE.

Prayer

Use the previous list and take a moment in quiet prayer. Pray over each item on your list and be completely candid with your Creator about your fears and shortcomings. He can handle them!

NEGLECT

Be careful that you do not forget the LORD, who brought you out of Egypt, out of the land of slavery.

Deuteronomy 6:12

Prayer isn't like fertilizing your lawn, which is indeed helpful to your grass but not absolutely necessary. Prayer is one of your soul's vital signs. It shows if your faith has a pulse.

Just as ungrateful children can get into the habit of just taking, taking, taking from generous parents, our prayer lives can suffer from neglect. We just forget. We put prayer off until later. We view it as a spiritual chore, like cleaning out the gutters, and defer it. We figure it can wait while we take care of important things.

Moses knew that his Israelites were susceptible to that same spiritual amnesia, forgetting who they were, forgetting how they were able to come so far, forgetting the One who was their very life. Shortly before he died, Moses urged them, "Be careful that you do not forget the LORD, who brought you out of Egypt, out of the land of slavery" (Deuteronomy 6:12).

Right now would be a great time to send a message to God to let him know how proud you are to be called his child.

Journaling Question

Have you ever stopped communicating with someone? What happened to that relationship as a result? Why do you think that is? Prayer is the way we communicate with God. What are some ways you can work more prayer time into your life?

Prayer

Dear Lord, I often act like an ungrateful child who never picks up the phone or writes but still expects to be taken care of. Help me be more mindful of my relationship with you. I am proud to be your child. Amen.

FEAR OF DISAPPOINTMENT

**Did I ask you for a son? . . . Didn't I tell you,
"Don't raise my hopes"?**

2 Kings 4:28

I have to admit that one thing that slows down my eagerness to pray is fear. I am afraid of being disappointed. Prayer, real prayer, honest prayer, involves opening up your heart, baring your feelings, taking a risk, exposing your tender side instead of the hardened armor we usually present to the world.

The prophet Elisha's intercession once brought a long-hoped-for son to an older woman. It was ecstasy to her soul; she had wanted so, so badly to be a mother. Then the boy grew sick and died in her arms. Mute with shock at first, she finally burst out in bitter distress, in "I knew it!" soul pain: "Did I ask you for a son? . . . Didn't I tell you, 'Don't raise my hopes'?" (2 Kings 4:28). It was Elisha's great privilege to channel God's life-giving power back into the boy, and he joyfully restored the boy to his mother.

But I know her fear, and you probably do too. Sometimes we may hesitate to ask God for something we desperately want or need because we assume we will be turned down.

Elisha's wonderful ministry helps us to trust that God always gets the last word, and his last word is always one of blessing, kindness, and victory. You don't have to be afraid to open your heart. Even if he lets you experience pain, the pain becomes the path to even greater joy.

Journaling Question

What are some of the thoughts and "asks" you desperately want to put into prayer but have held back out of fear of being disappointed?

Prayer

Dear God, you know what I most need in my life. Please hear me as I humbly pray for (insert your thoughts from the journaling question). I know I won't always get whatever I want in life. But I also know when that happens . . . you still have a plan for me. Amen.

SMALL FAITH

Why are you so afraid? Do you still have no faith?

Mark 4:40

Somebody observed once that you can tell how big a person's God is by how big his or her prayers are. Do you get the point? Do you agree? Whom do you worship? Is he omnipotent or semi-omnipotent? Is he the King and Lord of all or just the duke or earl of all? Is he the Master of the universe or merely a middle manager? Has Satan really been dealt a mortal blow, or is it just a flesh wound?

Jesus' disciples were once in a little boat during a mammoth storm. The boat was taking on water, and their God seemed small and remote. "Don't you care if we drown?" At just the right time Jesus looked at the waves and reminded them that they worked for him. "Be still!" He rebuked the furious winds, "Quiet!"

To the stunned disciples, Jesus commented sadly, **"Why are you so afraid? Do you still have no faith?"** (Mark 4:40). The upside is that experiences like this one helped their faith to mature and grow. Their memory of such extraordinary events served them well later in life when they were called on to risk their lives for the gospel.

How big is your faith? How big is your God? How big do you dare to pray?

Journaling Question

What are some "big" prayers you could make today? Our God is a big God; don't hesitate to ask!

/5/22 - 156 - pumpkin cheesecake
— KK eye appt today —
— 1 week before her move to dorm

Prayer

Dear God, sometimes I forget just how big you really are! In my shortsightedness, I forget all the amazing things you can accomplish. I often neglect to bring you my biggest burdens and live in fear as a result. Help me remember you are always in my boat—and in control of the storm! Amen.

MISPLACED PRIORITIES

**Seek first his kingdom and his righteousness,
and all these things will be given to you as well.**

Matthew 6:33

One of my persistent weaknesses is that I want to author my own play, the play of my life, in which I am the star, for which I would like to write the script. I can pretty much do fine on my own for a while, and then when I encounter a problem too big for me, I holler for God to show up on "my" stage, on my cue. He generally does not oblige me at such times. *Hmm.* Wonder why.

In the middle of his Sermon on the Mount, Jesus helped his disciples to see how the universe really operates. The more you grasp for material things, the more in love you are with yourself and your agenda, the less you will achieve and the less satisfaction you will feel.

Here is a better way: "Seek first his [God's] kingdom and his righteousness, and all these things will be given to you as well" (Matthew 6:33). Seeking God's kingdom means seeing yourself as God's creation, placed here on earth for a mission, *his* mission. You are in *his* play, and he will let you know the role he needs you to play for him.

Seeking God's righteousness means choosing to value your forgiveness of sins through the blood of Jesus as your most precious possession. When you have that, everything else that God thinks you need will come flowing into your life.

Journaling Question

What are some of the things you tend to prioritize ahead of your walk with God? Now write GOD at the top of that list and think about ways you can be more intentional about letting him take the lead in these areas.

6/22 - 171.ª - very bad - did yoga for 1 hr. yesterday - cheese & cracker, spaghetti (?)

Prayer

Dear Lord, instead of giving you first place in my life, I tend to prioritize (use the previous list to fill in this blank). Help me remember that being your child is my life's number-one blessing and that you will provide everything else that is necessary. Amen.

JUST TALK

The prayer of a righteous person is powerful and effective.

James 5:16

Maybe I'd pray more if it didn't look so weak. When I'm praying, I must look like I'm talking to myself, mumbling impossible things to nobody. Everybody craves a sign, power, and control, isn't it so? Wouldn't it have been cooler if upon becoming a Christian, you got a light saber to use? or blue lightning bolts? or a million dollars in gold ingots? Instead, God simply invites you to talk to him.

Talk is cheap, right? Maybe so, but not when you address your heavenly Father in the name of Jesus. Whether you speak your message out loud, sing it, whisper it, or just think it in your head, God hears you and guarantees to process your request.

What may look like a small person simply making weak sounds then becomes mighty. The apostle James has a simple, forceful, direct way of helping us understand God's ways. He says, "The prayer of a righteous person is powerful and effective" (James 5:16).

Did you grasp that? Every time you pray, you set something into motion. Every time you pray, something in the universe changes. You have never wasted a prayer in your life. Not a one falls to the ground unheard and unanswered. Your prayer talk makes you *powerful* and *effective* for God's work and your needs.

Journaling Question

Take a moment to describe your prayer life. What does it look like now? Where do you pray? Do you pray out loud or silently? with confidence or hesitation? How do you feel afterward?

1/7/22 — 116.(00) Did not eat after 8

Prayer

Dear heavenly Father, help me realize that even though my words may seem quiet and small, I can move mountains through prayer. You hear every word I think or say . . . and you answer every cry of my heart. Thank you, Father. Amen.

THE LORD'S PRAYER

Pastor Mark Jeske

THE ADDRESS

One day Jesus was praying in a certain place. When he finished, one of his disciples said to him, "Lord, teach us to pray, just as John taught his disciples." He said to them, "When you pray, say: '[Our] Father [in heaven].'"

Luke 11:1,2; Matthew 6:9

Jesus' public ministry lasted for three years. He spoke to many different people on many different occasions. The four gospels preserve only relatively small amounts of his precious words. He clearly spoke about the same topics in similar language at different times. Both Matthew and Luke record slightly different versions of the magnificent prayer he taught his friends to use.

"One day Jesus was praying in a certain place. When he finished, one of his disciples said to him, 'Lord, teach us to pray, just as John taught his disciples.' He said to them, 'When you pray, say: "[Our] Father [in heaven]"'" (Luke 11:1,2; Matthew 6:9).

The platform upon which all true prayer rests is to remember who you are and remember to whom you are speaking. You are addressing not an admiral or general, not a president or superhero, but your Father, your heavenly Father. You are related to him. He gave you birth and rebirth. He loves you more than you love your own children. You may claim his attention with childlike confidence because he has publicly claimed you through your baptism.

When you pray, you are not filling out a grant request to a heavenly charitable foundation. You are talking to your Father. And he loves taking care of his children.

Journaling Question

Take a moment to really think about the ideal parent/child relationship and what it entails. You have a heavenly Father who is not remote—but who loves you as dearly as his own kid. What does that mean to you? How does it make you feel? How does it make you want to live your life?

1/8/22 – 160 🙁 – Ate french fries after 9 pm.!!

Prayer

Dear heavenly Father, I can never fully understand the height and depth of your love for me. Thank you for loving me as your own dear child. Help me realize that because of your love, I have the full rights of being your child—and can talk to you in prayer, *whenever* and *however* I am able. Amen.

THE FIRST PETITION

Hallowed be your name.

Luke 11:2

To get more out of the praying experience, Jesus leads you away from you. Have you noticed how most of the petitions in his model prayer lead you to think about *God's* program instead of yours? It's not that material things are unimportant. It's that God's Word and ways are far more important.

Jesus' first sentence has only four words. Don't rush when you say them. They are a mouthful. "Hallowed be your name" (Luke 11:2). God's "name" refers not only to the various proper names that the Scripture reveals to us, like Lord or Christ. God's name in its fuller sense is his self-revelation. It's the sum of what we know about God's person and work.

The word *hallow* has mostly faded from contemporary English. It means "to consider holy." You can't make God any holier than he is already, can you? But you *can* ask for God's help to lift up his holiness in your heart and make him look good to the people around you in your life.

That means no idols. That means taking out the trash in your mind and recommitting yourself to the *one* Creator, *one* Savior, *one* Counselor. That means radiating the conviction to all around you, "I'm proud of my God."

Journaling Question

How can you reflect God's holiness to the people in your life?
Is there anything you can think about or pray for that would
elevate God's holiness in your own heart?

Prayer

Dear Lord, lift up your holiness in my heart so that I make you
the highest priority in my life. Help me reflect your light to
those living around me so that I live my life in a way that shows
how proud I am to be yours. Amen.

THE SECOND PETITION

When you pray, say: ". . . your kingdom come."

Luke 11:2

It is a mistake to think of God's kingdom as just a place. The whole earth is the Lord's, and the heavens too. The Bible uses the term to refer to Christ's ruling activity, his "reigning" in people's hearts through their faith in him. "When you pray, say: '. . . your kingdom come'" (Luke 11:2).

When you utter that powerful prayer, you are urging on the Holy Spirit to do his wonderful work of creating and strengthening faith in more and more people's hearts. You are also committing yourself to that mission as his field representative.

I guess you could say that this petition is a mission prayer. You are praying that hell will be emptier and heaven fuller. You are praying that the Spirit will claim minds and hearts where the darkness of Satan used to lie like a poisonous night fog. You are praying that people who are born, live, and die slaves of sin and Satan will become citizens of the kingdom of the light of Christ.

Every material thing that you can touch with your hands will soon be taken from you as you die. The only thing you can take with you to heaven is people. Pray for them. Help them find out how wonderful it is to belong to King Jesus.

Journaling Question

The only thing we can take to heaven is people—not our accomplishments or any "stuff" we've collected along the way—but PEOPLE. Who are some people who desperately need praying for in your life? Write down their names as well as some specific thoughts about how you could pray for them.

10/22 – 161 – fruit salad – family dinner after Kevin + Wonnie got sick.

Francis – skin lesions due to covid
Jennifer – peace in her life
Francesca – quarantine – fever
Lizel + Juan –
Mom + Grammy –
KK – school
Kirsten + Banks – NC
Kevin + Wonnie – Mexico
Bob – back / shoulder pain
Neng – repose of her soul
Papa – recovery
Mary and siblings – recovery + peace

Prayer

Take a moment to pray over the people in your list above. Ask God to make you a light in their lives, leading them toward his glory.

THE THIRD PETITION

**When you pray, say: ". . . your will be done,
on earth as it is in heaven."**

Luke 11:2; Matthew 6:10

"When you pray, say: '. . . your will be done, on earth as it is in heaven'" (Luke 11:2; Matthew 6:10). Doesn't this sound backward? You come to God in prayer to tell him what you want, and then Jesus says that a better way is to come to God in prayer and first ask him what *he* wants.

Wise counsel. The point is that you won't know what is good for you until you are tuned into his goodness. You won't know what is the smart thing to pray for until you are first tuned into his wisdom.

Jesus modeled this humble, healthy attitude all the way to the cross. As he himself fought the terrible spiritual struggle to stay committed to the plan that he offer up his life, he went to his Father in prayer in the Garden of Gethsemane. He prayed, "Not my will but yours be done." The result was a strengthened resolve that led to Satan's crushing defeat and forgiveness won for the whole world.

The greatest and most satisfying moments in your life will occur when you are carrying out God's will as his joyful agent on earth.

Journaling Question

Describe a time in your life when you prayed for something
but God gave you something else. What did you learn from the
experience?

1/11/22 - 120 😊 - No food after dinner except
peanuts

Prayer

Dear God, I know I often come to you with a list of things *I'd* like
to see happen in my life. Help me realize that when I seek *your*
will instead of mine, amazing things will happen! Amen.

THE FOURTH PETITION

When you pray, say: ". . . Give us each day our daily bread."

Luke 11:2,3

Finally—Jesus invites us to ask for material things. After reorienting our priorities to put God on the throne of our lives, recommitting ourselves to his saving agenda, and vowing obedience to his will, we are ready to talk about physical things. "When you pray, say: '. . . Give us each day our daily bread'" (Luke 11:2,3).

It is a delightful practice to pray when sitting down to eat. It is totally appropriate that we give God credit for so richly and consistently supplying us with not only bread but all our food. Soil, rainfall, seeds, and sunshine all come from him. It is humbling but accurate to see God as the originator of every meal you eat.

"Daily bread" is also a metaphor for everything that you need to have a healthy and productive life. Jesus' choice of the lowly word *bread* is a reminder that God obligates himself to give you everything he thinks you need, though perhaps not everything you want.

Daily is also an allusion to the Israelites' *manna*, the miracle bread that appeared every day while they lived in the wilderness after the exodus from Egypt. "Daily bread" reminds us that God generally doesn't front us our supplies a year in advance. He prefers to dribble them out on an as-needed basis.

Journaling Question

Daily bread is a metaphor for anything you need for a healthy life. Make a list of some of the daily bread items you are thankful for and another list of daily bread items you would like to receive.

12/22 - 126 ☺ Did not eat after 9 pm

Prayer

Craft a prayer around your two lists. Take the time to thank God genuinely for all the blessings he showers upon you, and then humbly ask him for the things you need.

THE FIFTH PETITION

**When you pray, say: ". . . Forgive us our sins,
for we also forgive everyone who sins against us."**

Luke 11:2,4

Only Christianity gives it away.

Every human being who has ever lived has a conscience and knows two things for sure: there is evil within me, and I am in some kind of trouble with the holy Power out there. When people make up their own religious systems, they always put the pressure on the individual to make amends. There are rules to keep, rituals to observe, propitiations and sacrifices, pilgrimages, and various acts of devotion and obedience. But only Christianity *gives* forgiveness away. Jesus invites you to ask for it.

"When you pray, say: '. . . Forgive us our sins, for we also forgive everyone who sins against us'" (Luke 11:2,4). Jesus Christ, on Calvary's cross, did all the obeying, sacrificing, and paying that was necessary. He bought forgiveness of sins for the whole world, and everyone who believes it has it. He gives it away.

He also charges his believers to show that same mercy to the fools and sinners who surround them each day. How can the first half of that prayer be so easy and the second half so hard? When you pray the Fifth Petition, pray it with all your might. Don't let Satan steal your absolute confidence of forgiveness, and don't let a shabby spirit withhold that same forgiveness to people who ask it of you.

Journaling Question

Sometimes being forgiven is so much easier than having to forgive! Describe a time when you had trouble forgiving someone.
Why was it so hard? How do you feel about it now?

1/23/22 —126 — woke up in WY— on
the way to VA Tech for KK's
move

Prayer

Dear Lord, sometimes it is so very hard to do the right thing
and forgive others—especially when someone hurts me deeply.
Help me remember your amazing act of forgiveness—for me
and all the world—on the cross. And give me strength to offer
forgiveness to others. Amen.

THE SIXTH PETITION

When you pray, say: ". . . lead us not into temptation."

Luke 11:2,4

Your heavenly Father watches your progress on the road to everlasting life and eagerly desires your success. He takes no delight in watching some fall away. Jesus urges you to ask the Father's help in staying strong: "When you pray, say: '. . . lead us not into temptation'" (Luke 11:2,4).

James 1:13 shows us that God never tempts anyone to sin; he hates the very notion. The five little words in this petition are shorthand for a plea that God would have mercy on us because of our many sinful weaknesses and keep us from committing spiritual suicide. We are all prone to becoming careless, stubborn, hard of hearing, and reckless in the way we live, and we must keep imploring God to send his angels of protection.

You can help God answer that prayer. The Bible is a mighty resource to keep us out of temptation. It is armor for our hearts and a helmet for our brains. I hope you read some of it each day. He also sends other Christian people into your life—listen to them when they speak words of warning to you.

One of God's greatest gifts to you is your congregation. Cherish it and thank God for the strength you draw from it. Your pastor cares about your spiritual well-being, prays for your safe journey, and will help you watch out for the ditches.

Journaling Question

Life is full of temptations! What are a few temptations in your life that seem hard to resist?

1-14-22 — Woke up at the Marriott —
KK moves in today

Prayer

Dear God, thank you for giving me churches, pastors, and your Holy Word to help me in my fight against temptation. I know you want the best for me. Thank you for the strength you freely offer so that I am not alone and can resist temptation daily. Amen.

THE SEVENTH PETITION

When you pray, say: ". . . deliver us from the evil one."

Luke 11:2; Matthew 6:13

Call me naïve, but I'd like to think that I don't have any enemies. I mean real enemies—people who would like to assault or kill me.

That's what Satan would like me to think. The Bible calls him a dragon, a lion, a serpent, always prowling about looking for people to devour. He is indeed a deadly enemy. He would like to attack us physically; invade our minds; re-enslave our wills; and trap us forever in the burning, sulfurous dungeon that is his destiny.

"When you pray, say: '. . . deliver us from the evil one'" (Luke 11:2; Matthew 6:13). Mean this when you pray it. The words *devil* and *hell* have lost much of their meaning in the way people talk today. They are joke words, rude emphasis words. But they contain a deadly reality—that the prince of darkness is seeking whom he may devour, and he's coming for you.

Jesus crushed the serpent's head when he died and rose again. All people who trust in him as their Savior are forgiven and immortal, safe and secure. Claim your forgiveness from Christ, grow in knowledge and power from the Word, and pray for the final deliverance. When you are in heaven, you will never need to pray this petition again.

Journaling Question

The words *devil* and *hell* have lost a little bit of their punch. How does today's culture (television/movies/social customs) view the devil and hell? How does the Bible describe them? Do you notice a difference?

1/5/22 - 150 !! cookies - ☺
— KK has moved in + slept in dorm

Prayer

Dear Jesus, help me be aware of the serious threat the devil and hell represent. Satan is not a harmless cartoon character with a pitchfork . . . but rather an insidious enemy. But you are so much more powerful! Thank you, God, for defeating death and hell! Help me awaken others to the knowledge of this truth. Amen.

THE DOXOLOGY

Worthy is the Lamb, who was slain, to receive power and wealth and wisdom and strength and honor and glory and praise!

Revelation 5:12

The conclusion to the Lord's Prayer as we speak it in church is not found in the Bible. Protestants almost universally end it by saying, "The kingdom and the power and the glory are yours, now and forever."

Even though that *doxology* (a statement of praise to the Trinity) is not in the Bible's prayer, it still makes a great finishing statement to Jesus' teaching. It explains why we have confidence that all we ask for will be granted. It reaffirms our promise to make the Lord's name hallowed, work to extend his gracious rule in people's hearts, and make obedience to his will a life priority.

St. John heard a magnificent song from angels who surround the throne of God: "Worthy is the Lamb, who was slain, to receive power and wealth and wisdom and strength and honor and glory and praise!" (Revelation 5:12).

A doxology like that one is a great way to end any prayer:

• We affirm that God is our supreme Ruler, our King.

• We affirm that God is able to do all we ask and more.

• We pledge to give him all honor and glory.

And when you say "Amen" at the end, you put your personal exclamation point on what you just said. "That's the truth!"

Journaling Question

Why do you think it's important to have a doxology at the end of a prayer, such as the Lord's Prayer does?

1/16/22 – 154 – Carbs
— Back home 4 inches of snow

Write your own doxology here:

Prayer

Dear heavenly Father, you are my supreme King! Thank you for being able to do immeasurably more than I could ever ask or imagine. All honor and glory are yours! Amen.

HOW TO PRAY

Pastor Mike Novotny

OUR *FATHER*

This, then, is how you should pray: "Our Father in heaven."

Matthew 6:9

I never thought I would be the guy to stare at children while they sleep. But I do. When I get home late from work or from soccer, I sneak into my daughters' bedrooms and I just stare. Sometimes I sit down on the carpet and just look at their bare feet sticking out from the fuzzy pink blankets. Or I fix my eyes on their little faces snuggled up against their favorite "stuffy." There are few things more beautiful or more emotional for me than those two girls.

Which is why I adore Jesus' prayer. When his disciples begged him for a tutorial on talking to God, Jesus didn't say, "Pray like this—Our King in heaven." Nor did he instruct them to say, "Our Judge in heaven." No, he gave them a pattern for prayer that stirs our hearts. Jesus said, "This, then, is how you should pray: 'Our *Father* in heaven'" (Matthew 6:9). What a word! God is your *Father*. You are his child. Incredible, isn't it?

After all you've done wrong. After all you've failed to do right. After all you've struggled with, indulged in, or been too scared to stand up for. After all of it, God is not ashamed to call you his kid. He feels the way I feel when I sit on the carpet and stare at my kids. Love swells up in his heart. Emotion floods his mind. You are not a minion to God. Not a name or a number. You are infinitely valuable. If you could only see your Father's face when he looks down upon you!

Journaling Question

How is praying, "Dear Father in heaven" different from praying, "Dear King in heaven"? Or, "Dear Judge in heaven"? How does this parent/child relationship affect the way you come to God in prayer?

1-17/22 -150

Prayer

Dear Lord, I know you love me like a father . . . and that love floods your heart when you think of me. Please help me remember and value this priceless relationship between us every day. Amen.

OUR FATHER *IN HEAVEN*
(part 1)

Our Father in heaven.

Matthew 6:9

I accidentally threw my dad under the bus the other day. I was trying to tell a fictional, first-person story about a guy with a bad father, so I said, "I never had a dad who was loving . . ." The church got awkwardly quiet. They thought I was talking about my own father. Even worse, my dad goes to our church!

By God's grace, I had (and still have) a really good dad. He traveled crazy distances to watch me play soccer. He supported my desire for ministry even before he was a churchgoing guy. And he is a wonderful grandpa to my girls.

But I know not everyone has a dad like that. Maybe your dad was demanding and gruff. Maybe he was ashamed of you. Maybe he was a hypocrite who went to church, went home, and hurt your mom. Maybe he showed up for your conception and then bailed for the rest of your story.

If so, I want to introduce you to a prayer Jesus taught. It starts, "Our Father in heaven" (Matthew 6:9). I love those last two words—*in heaven*. Our God is not an earthly father. Not a flawed, sinful man who fails us in scarring ways. No, God is a Father who is in heaven, where sin cannot exist. He is holy. It is impossible for him to break a promise to you.

Pray that prayer often. Say those words slowly. Having a great father can change your life in powerful ways. Thankfully, you have one. Because he is not just our Father. He is our Father *in heaven*.

Journaling Question

List some of the attributes of a great father. Perhaps your earthly dad had all these attributes. Maybe he didn't. But your HEAVENLY Father exceeds them all!

1/7/22 - 178 - should fast 10 hrs before nothing to eat after 9 pm

1/18/22 - 114 - even had Tenn bar!

Prayer

Dear God, thank you for being such a loving Father. Thank you for never breaking a single promise that you have made and for loving me in a way that no one else can. Amen.

OUR FATHER *IN HEAVEN*
(part 2)

Our Father in heaven.

Matthew 6:9

My daughters are still at that priceless stage where they adore their daddy. When I come home from work, they drop everything and sprint, squealing, to squeeze their arms around Daddy's legs. (They'll do that when they're 16, right?) They love their father. Why wouldn't they? I have loved them first, in a million different ways.

Loving God can be a bit more challenging. Because even Jesus admitted that we pray to "our Father in heaven" (Matthew 6:9). *In heaven* means he's not on earth. He's not visible or touchable. Therefore, believing our Father loves us and accepts us despite our sins can be a great challenge for our faith.

That is precisely why our Father gives fathers . . . and mothers . . . and friends. Good people are great glimpses of the best Father. Whenever your dad lends you some money in your time of need. Whenever your mom lends her ear and just listens to your struggles. Whenever your friends make you laugh and invite you to hang out. Every time someone on earth is kind, patient, selfless, and forgiving, they are helping us to know, in a deeply personal way, the expression that is on our heavenly Father's face.

Today you will not be able to see your Father. Unless you see by faith. By faith, you see God's face when you look at their faces, a glimpse of his glory. Now I'm off to give two little girls a glimpse of their Father who is in heaven. They can't yet see his face, but they can see mine.

Journaling Question

Make a list of some of the most important people in your life. Now list a few of their amazing attributes . . . words that describe what they do for you and how they help you through life. These are ALL expressions of God's face!

−19-22 − 140 − Doritos !

Prayer

Take some time to pray over the list of people above. Thank your heavenly Father for all the people he puts in your life and the many ways they show God's face to you on a daily basis.

OUR FATHER IN HEAVEN

Our Father in heaven.

Matthew 6:9

Once upon a time, Billy had the best dad. Billy's dad valued his family more than his career. He leveraged those early years, the ones that pass so quickly, to shape his son with God's love and give the boy a glimpse of God the Father—present, kind, forgiving, encouraging. Billy grew up loved, protected, and blessed by his dad.

What do you feel as you read about Billy's father? I'm guessing something like, "Good for Billy." Because stories about even the best fathers mean nothing to us when it's *his* father or *her* father or *their* father. The only father that means much to us is *our* father.

Which is why I love Jesus' prayer. He taught us to pray, "*Our* Father in heaven" (Matthew 6:9). That has to be the most beautiful possessive pronoun in the history of grammar! This ever-present, always-compassionate, relentlessly forgiving Father is *our* Father. We are his children. You are his dear daughter. You are his precious son.

Do you know what that means? If you tried to call up Warren Buffet and ask for money, he wouldn't take your call. He's not your father. But if you called to God in prayer and asked for anything in Jesus' name—for endurance against cancer, for the ability to forgive your critics, for courage to share your faith—he would listen. He would give you his full attention. He would care. He would either give you exactly what you wanted or something even better. That's the power of having *our* Father in heaven.

Journaling Question

How does it make you feel that the most amazing Father in all of creation is YOUR Father? Your *heavenly* Father! Take a little time to reflect on what that means for you as you walk through the hills and valleys of life. What do you have to fear? How can you respond to challenges?

Prayer

Dear Lord, thank you for being my Father—the *BEST* Father! I know I can call on you at any time—during my highs and lows—and you will answer. You are never too busy or too limited to give me your full attention. I love you, Father. Amen.

HALLOWED BE YOUR NAME

Our Father in heaven, hallowed be your name.

Matthew 6:9

Hallowed be thy name. Recognize those words? They are the second line (and the first request) in the most famous prayer of all time, the Lord's Prayer. But do you know what they mean? (Would you bet your smartphone on your answer?) *Hallowed?* Not exactly a word we use, well, ever! Is it like . . . *Hallow-een?* Is it . . . the way British gentlemen greet one another? Hallow! Isn't it . . . the name of the last Harry Potter book?

Let me help. *Hallowed* is a verb that technically means "to honor as sacred." But I prefer this definition—"to think of someone as wonderfully different." In this case, God's name (what we think about God). That helps me understand Jesus' famous prayer. The very first thing to pray for, even before daily bread and forgiveness of sins, is for help to think of our Father as wonderfully different. Because if I think of God as different from everything I love in this life, as infinitely better than the best parts of my days, then my soul gets stirred up to worship.

Like this—"Father, open my eyes to see that you are more beautiful than the sun coming up. You are more faithful than my golden retriever. You are more exciting than a last-second touchdown pass. You are more captivating than the little toes of my newborn granddaughter. You are more enjoyable than perfectly cooked pasta. You are more forgiving than my best friend. In a million ways, Father, you are more. You are different. Wonderfully different."

That's what Jesus meant when he taught, "Our Father in heaven, hallowed be your name" (Matthew 6:9).

Journaling Question

Make a list of some of your favorite things in life. This can include people, activities, or meals . . . anything you can think of!

Prayer

Take a moment in prayer to recognize that of all those things you just listed above, God is more perfect—and more wonderfully different—than all of them! Tell God how much that means to you. Write your prayer here.

PRAY THE NAME

Hallowed be your name.

Matthew 6:9

When I was a kid, I learned a way to pray called the A.C.T.S. Method. It stood for Adoration, Confession, Thanksgiving, and Supplication (asking for stuff). I understood the "I'm sorrys" and "thank you fors" and "please gimmes," but I never really got that first part. Adoration?

But now I get why the Lord's Prayer starts there. Adore God. Hallow his name. Meditate on how wonderfully different God is from even the best things in your life. Pray, "God, you are glorious. You created all of this. Your love never fails. You never change. You are always faithful, always forgiving, always in control. You are my hidden treasure, my everything. Earth has nothing I desire besides you."

If you start there, do you know what so naturally comes next? Confession. "But, God, that makes my sin even worse. I forgot your name. I ran to _____ to make me happy instead of to you." And do you know what flows from there? Thanksgiving. "But, Jesus, there is forgiveness in your name! You knew what I would do, but you still died for a sinner like me." Finally, supplication gets spiritual. "God, I want to have a good day, but what I really want is you. I want to remember you, know you, and see you by faith. I don't need anything else. Neither do my friends, my kids, my family. So, God, please open our minds to see you as wonderfully different as you are. 'Hallowed be your name' (Matthew 6:9). Amen!"

Oh, that's a great way to pray!

Journaling Question

Using the A.C.T.S. Method, write down some thoughts for a personal prayer. Start with adoration . . . confession, thanksgiving, and supplication.

_____

_____

_____

_____

_____

_____

_____

_____

_____

_____

_____

_____

Prayer

Now that you've written down your thoughts (above), take a few quiet moments to pray about them. Tell God what's on your heart and mind.

P.R.A.Y.

Praise be to the God and Father of our Lord Jesus Christ!

1 Peter 1:3

Most of my prayers sounds like this: "Dear God, AAAAAAAAAAAAAA! In Jesus' name. Amen."

I should explain. I think of prayer as having four steps—Praise. Repent. Ask. Yield. (P.R.A.Y.) But my prayers tend to jump to and stay focused on the third step—Ask. "Dear God, please bless this and fix that and be with them." How about you? Do you focus on the Ask when you pray?

Peter offers an encouragement not to skip the praise. He begins, "Praise be to the God and Father of our Lord Jesus Christ!" (1 Peter 1:3). Before asking for God to fix his friends' suffering, Peter pushes his friends to praise God in the midst of their suffering.

Here's why—Once we Praise, our prayers change. Once we spend quality (and quantity!) time saying good things about God's love, God's power, God's holiness, God's wisdom, God's control, God's presence, and God's character, our prayers evolve. We immediately start to Repent: "God, you are so good to me, yet I chose to do something bad against you . . ." And we Ask: "God, if people only knew how good you are, doctor visits and medical bills and loneliness couldn't stop their joy. So open their eyes to know you better!" And we Yield: "God, you know everything, and you want what's best for me, so I trust you. I'm asking for this, but your will be done."

Can I challenge you for the next 24 hours to begin every prayer with a word of praise?

Journaling Question

Write some thoughtful, personal praise for God—directly from you to him. If you need help, think about how you feel about God's character, his presence, his wisdom, and his love. Describe those attributes of God and how they make you feel. Praise your Lord!

_____

_____

_____

_____

_____

Prayer

Use the thoughts you wrote above to start a prayer to God. Beginning with your heartfelt, personal words of praise, let the prayer blossom from there into a moment for repentance, asking, and yielding.

_____

_____

_____

_____

THE MAN WHO PREACHED TO 20 MILLION

**Going a little farther, [Jesus] fell with his face
to the ground and prayed.**

Matthew 26:39

One day a reporter went to witness the most famous man on earth in action. Walter Maier, the Lutheran radio preacher whose sermons reached 40,000,000 ears every week, was about to record another message. When the reporter arrived at the studio, however, he didn't see Maier. He looked into the recording booth and saw nothing but an empty room. But the tour guide smiled at the reporter, "Look down." The reporter took a step closer and saw the celebrity on the floor of the studio, on his face, begging God to bless his message.

I love that story. It reminds us all to stay humble, no matter how successful we are in ministry, business, or life. Even more, it reminds us of Jesus. Despite the notoriety and the size of his miracle-seeking crowds, where do we find Jesus at the end of his life? Matthew tells us, "Going a little farther, [Jesus] fell with his face to the ground and prayed" (Matthew 26:39).

Jesus stayed humble. As our sinless Savior, he avoided the proud assumption that he could handle things without prayer. Thus, when he died the next day, he had a perfect life to give for you, a sacrifice that would make God's face shine with approval every time he thought of you.

So imitate Maier as you humbly pray today, and worship your Savior for praying his way to your salvation!

Journaling Question

Why do you think it's so hard to stay humble in your day-to-day life? When do you find yourself forgetting to stay humble? Why is an attitude of humbleness important?

Guide me this week, Lord, and show me how to go about ALL my tasks. When I feel overwhelmed, I pray that you will touch my shoulder to remind me of your presence and the power of your word.

This I ask in Jesus' name,
Amen.

Prayer

Dear Lord, you humbled yourself in unbelievable ways for me on your journey to the cross. Teach me to be humble no matter how much success I have in life. Amen.

NOT UNTIL YOU BLESS ME

Then the man said, "Let me go, for it is daybreak." But Jacob replied, "I will not let you go unless you bless me."

Genesis 32:26

It's not insulting to be demanding with God. Some Christians, in a desire to be humble, turn all their prayers into question marks, into soul-numbing, expecting-little "God willings." But there are times when your prayers should be much bolder. There are times when you should be demanding with God.

Think of the strange night when Jacob wrestled with God, who was disguised as a man: "Then the man said, 'Let me go, for it is daybreak.' But Jacob replied, 'I will not let you go unless you bless me'" (Genesis 32:26). Jacob wouldn't let God race off to his morning appointment. Instead, his fingers clamped onto God's arms. With a dislocated hip, Jacob had to be clinging desperately to him. Yet in that desperation, Jacob demanded, "Don't you even think about walking away until you do something good for me." And God did. Instead of being insulted, he was honored. Jacob was clinging to God's promise, believing that God could not lie like his mother, Rebekah, or his Uncle Laban. Jacob believed God was faithful.

God is faithful to you too. What God said about being with you right now has to be true (Matthew 28:20). What he said about working out all things for your good, even that painful thing, has to be true (Romans 8:28). What he said about forgiving all your sins, not just the ones people talk about at Bible study, has to be true (1 John 1:9). So cling to God. Insist on his character. Refuse to let him go until he blesses you.

Journaling Question

It's okay to be demanding sometimes when we talk to God, not in a greedy way but in a way that shows just how forcefully we believe every word God tells us! What are some things you would like to pray *forcefully* today?

Pray for Uncle Randall's soul.
Pray for his family
Pray for my family in Philippines
- Pray for Bob + the kids
- Pray for Bob's family

Prayer

Use your answer above to craft a prayer to God here:

Lord, help me to be an example for my children, reveal your grace + power to them, Lord.

Thank you, Lord, I made it another week, another good week! I need to sell one more home, I pray - lead the right person to me.

BUT GOD SAID

[The LORD] is faithful in all he does.

Psalm 33:4

I once made the mistake of promising my kids more than I could deliver. At the start of a lazy Saturday, I said, "Girls, today we are going to eat lunch and take naps and do the Slip and Slide and make dinner and read the Bible and watch a movie and play some board games." But, as I should have guessed, we couldn't fit in everything that Daddy planned. When bedtime arrived, before the board games were out, want to guess what my kids whined? "But, Dad! You said!"

It's hard to admit, but we are all less than faithful to our promises. Most of the time we don't intend it, but it still happens. We make a promise, but then something comes up that we didn't know about. Or we run out of time or energy and have to change the plans.

But this is one more reason I love God. Psalm 33:4 praises, "[The LORD] is faithful in all he does." Because God knows everything (nothing surprises him) and because God can do anything (he never runs out of energy), he keeps every promise he makes. He is faithful. So when he promises that your prayers are more than token religious habits, he means it. When he assures you that your time in his Word will never come back empty, he means it. A faithful God couldn't mean anything less.

So hold your Father to his Word. Insist, with the faith of a child, "But, God, you said!"

Journaling Question

What are some of the promises (big or small) you've made in your life? Were they hard to keep? Why is it sometimes hard to keep promises?

1/26/22

Tithe – I haven't taken the time to do it this month

Prayer

Dear Lord, I know you keep every single promise you make. Help me remember that I can lean on your faithfulness at every moment in my life. You will never let me down! Amen.

COME, LORD JESUS

Amen. Come, Lord Jesus.

Revelation 22:20

Every few days, my family uses a common prayer before eating dinner. It starts, "Come, Lord Jesus, be our guest . . ." I like that line. I try to envision Jesus answering that prayer, walking into the room, and joining us with his life-giving, happiness-increasing presence. The thought of him makes me happier than the food at the table or the people sitting around it.

But that prayer is not reserved for just the evening meal. It's the deepest and most constant cry of every Christian heart. The Bible's second to last verse says, "Amen. Come, Lord Jesus" (Revelation 22:20). Because when Jesus comes in glory on the Last Day, everything bad and broken will have to leave. Everything we regret and fear will be dead and gone. Everything we long for and desire will be ours forever. Can you imagine a life like that?

No more sadness, loneliness, or restlessness. No more disabilities, disease, or death. No grief, no fears, no phobias. No addictions, no compulsions, no obsessions. No PTSD, OCD, STD, or ADHD. No triggers, no trauma, no trying just to get by. Only glory. Only a happiness we have never felt. Only a rest that finally lets us sit and breathe and beam with joy. This is our hope. That is our for-sure future. It is going to happen. It sometimes feels like forever away, but soon and very soon we will see Jesus.

Amen! Come, Lord Jesus! Come quickly!

Journaling Question

When Jesus comes, all the cares and ills of this world will fall away. The broken will be made new. What does this mean for you personally? What things will be made perfect for you? What will you NOT have to worry or stress about anymore? Jot it down. How does it make you feel to think of this burden lifting when Christ comes?

1/27/22 – Jenny's 53rd – sent her
              basket
        – special prayer for her birthday

Prayer

Pray over your list above. Tell Christ what you're looking forward to when he comes again in glory. Thank him for the joy that will be yours when that day arrives!

PRAY FOR THE CHILDREN

**How good and pleasant it is when
God's people live together in unity!**

Psalm 133:1

Ever heard of what happens to pastors' daughters? I have. And it freaks me out. The other night I snuck into my daughter's room and knelt at the side of her bed. Her pigtails poked out as her little face snuggled into a sea of stuffed animals. I smiled. And I prayed. Because I know it's coming. With big girl height and big girl teeth come big girl desires. As much as I want to threaten every boy who talks to her with the thickest leather-bound German Bible I can find, I know I can't. That's how pastors' daughters go wild.

So what do I do instead? I pray. I pray for the boy who will one day catch her eye. I pray he knows God. The God who gives. The God who forgives. The God who died so he could live. And I pray for his parents. I pray they show him what happens when Jesus is at the center, when a guy leads by asking, "How can I help?" I pray, and then I go to hold the hand of the woman who worships with me every day. I think of the psalmist's words, "How good and pleasant it is when God's people [including husbands and wives] live together in unity!" (Psalm 133:1).

Could you start praying today? For your son or daughter? Your niece or your nephew? The little kids you give high fives to at church? Maybe you can help lead them to the only place that truly is happily ever after—the presence of God.

Journaling Question

Make a list of some of the children in your life, even if they're just children you see in the community or at church. How can you pray for them today?

- Keiaura
- Kristen
- Kevin
- Francesca
- Cara
- Neeya
- Justin

Prayer

Dear heavenly Father, bless all the little children! Help me be a light to them so they can see you through me. Please bless their futures and keep their feet on the path of your Word. (Take a moment to pray specifically for the children you listed above). Amen.

PRAY FOR THE PERSECUTED CHURCH

If one part suffers, every part suffers with it.

1 Corinthians 12:26

According to Open Doors USA, an organization that tracks Christian persecution around our planet, 245 million believers face threats, violence, and death every day because of their connection to Jesus. That's 1 in 9 global Christians. Like Leah who was abducted in Nigeria with one hundred of her classmates for refusing to convert to Islam. Or Maizah whose conversion to Christianity meant she was beaten and forced to become the fourth wife of her abuser unless she wanted to watch her family die. Or the Christians in rural China whose neighbors are offered money by the atheistic government for reporting any followers of Jesus that they know.

What can you do? Pray. Paul wrote, "If one part [of the church] suffers, every part suffers with it" (1 Corinthians 12:26). Pray for the persecuted church. Right now these suffering Christians are somewhere thinking something. Pray that Leah thinks of the eternity of pleasure Jesus has promised and not the brutal pain that will one day end. Pray that Maizah remembers the sermons she has heard and the passages she has believed. Pray for every church that gathers on Sunday with the threats of their neighbors in their ears. Pray they would not be afraid of those who can only kill the body. Pray they would fix their thoughts on Jesus, the Savior who has promised that those who stand firm will receive the crown of life.

Jesus, come quickly and rescue your church! And help us to pray for each other until that day comes!

Journaling Question

So many Christians around the world are persecuted. Take a moment to reflect on what it means to you to be able to worship freely and without fear. Is this something you take for granted? Can you imagine life if the opposite were true?

Prayer

Dear Lord, I can't imagine what it would be like to suffer for my faith, but millions of people do! Please be with those believers who face daily persecution and pain for their beliefs. Walk with them. Hold them close. Help me not take my ability to worship you for granted. Amen.

HOW DO I FORGIVE?

Father . . . we also forgive everyone who sins against us.

Luke 11:2,4

Years ago I got into a rather unloving exchange with a fellow Christian. The tension had been growing for months, so we met face-to-face to figure it out. As we talked about what God would want us to do—just love—she closed her eyes and gave a slow nod: "I know . . . I know . . ." I sighed because I knew exactly how she felt. As a Christian, I wanted to let it go and choose to love her as the Bible commands. But it can be so hard to get the truth of the Word into the emotions of your heart, the thoughts of your mind, and the words of your lips.

Have you felt that too?

If so, Jesus wants to help. That's why he taught us to pray, "Father . . . we also forgive everyone who sins against us" (Luke 11:2,4). Our Savior knew how hard forgiveness would be, so he directed us to the source of supernatural power. When you feel like you can't, talk to the God who always can!

But look at what Jesus said first: "Forgive us *our sins*, for we also forgive everyone who sins against us" (Luke 11:4). "First, Father, forgive us our sins. Forgive me mine." Forgiveness starts not with you forgiving them but with God forgiving you. And he has! And he is! And he will!

So when forgiving them seems impossible, remember to pray to your supremely capable and shockingly forgiving Father.

Journaling Question

Do you remember a time when it was hard to forgive someone? Jot down a few thoughts. Why was it hard to forgive? What finally made it easier? Do you still struggle with it? How does God's forgiveness of all *your* sins make it easier to forgive those who hurt you?

2/11/22

Prayer

Dear God, forgiveness isn't always easy, especially when I've been hurt badly. Help me remember your forgiveness of my sins—yesterday, today, and even tomorrow—and help me be humble and forgive others who have hurt me. Amen.

WHEN YOU CAN'T, HE CAN

[Jesus] got up and rebuked the winds and the waves, and it was completely calm.

Matthew 8:26

There comes a time in your life when you can't. Despite all your efforts, you can't control a situation in your family or you can't solve a problem with your health or you can't work things out with your siblings. The *USS Independence* is sinking, and you simply can't.

But God can! That's what Matthew learned the day when "[Jesus] got up and rebuked the winds and the waves, and it was completely calm" (Matthew 8:26). Can you even imagine this? Jesus wiped his groggy eyes, lifted his divine voice, and shook a commanding finger at the storm . . . and it listened! From grown men screaming for help to a silence so still you could hear Matthew's breath. "Why are you so afraid?" Jesus can!

Please don't forget that. While we might not know God's will or understand his timing, we do know his power. So we can pray, "God, you can bring a good friend into my life today. You can save this marriage, even this marriage, this year. You can change my unrealistic expectations. You can give me peace on unproductive days. You can make my pet sins a part of my past. You can give me the faith to forgive him. You can transform me into a patient parent. You can overcome this addiction. God, you can cure cancer. You can defeat depression. You can leave doctors dumbfounded. You're God! You're the omnipotent, all-powerful, can-do-anything God who can calm any storm."

Pray with boldness as you keep the faith that God can.

Journaling Question

What are some circumstances you have faced or are facing in your life that often feel overwhelming?

Prayer

Dear God, I can never understand fully your marvelous ways. But I do know that whenever I face seemingly impossible difficulties in my life, you can do ALL things. Please help me with (insert any issues you may have listed above or thank God for helping you in the past). Amen.

THE KEY TO GREAT PRAYER

**Whoever takes the lowly position of this child
is the greatest in the kingdom of heaven.**

Matthew 18:4

A few weeks ago, I asked our church a dangerous question: "What grade would you give your prayer life?" About 160 people gave their mostly uninspiring answers: C+, D, B, D-. "My prayer life lacks intentionality." "My mind is always distracted." Most people longed to be better at prayer.

I can relate to that. Over the years, I've preached on prayer, read books on prayer, and set goals around prayer, but I'm not there with prayer. Not close to where I want to be in my daily conversations with my Father.

But recently, God showed me the key to a great prayer life. It happened while I was studying Jesus' words: "Whoever takes the lowly position of this child is the greatest in the kingdom of heaven" (Matthew 18:4). What is it about children that makes them so great in Jesus' eyes? Answer—They know they are helpless. The reason little kids cry, "Mommy!" a hundred times a day is because they don't have the skills to cook lunch, the money to buy toys, or the height to see over the grown-ups. Their helplessness forces them to ask for help.

Light. Bulb. Moment. When we remember that we are helpless without God, it forces us to pray humbly. "God, without you I can't love my brother. Or raise this daughter. Or forgive my ex. Or make my friend a Christian. Or escape this shame. Or say no to this sin. Or trust you in this tragedy. I need you, God. Every day, I need you."

Remembering our lowly position—as helpless humans—will keep us talking to God in prayer.

Journaling Question

What grade would you give your prayer life? Why? Would you like to see this change? Why? Better yet . . . how?

FEB. 1, 2022 !

Prayer

Dear Lord, I am helpless without you—completely, utterly helpless. But that's okay! Because it helps me rely totally on you. Help me remember this when I'm feeling beaten and low. I am your child, and you are always holding out your hand to help me. Thank you, Father! Amen.

POWERFUL PRAYERS ARE . . .

Pastor Mark Jeske

BOLD

Ask and it will be given to you; seek and you will find; knock and the door will be opened to you. For everyone who asks receives; the one who seeks finds; and to the one who knocks, the door will be opened.

Matthew 7:7,8

"I am Oz, the great and terrible," the wizard face roared above the flames. "Who are you, whippersnapper?"

"I am Dorothy, the small and meek," she replied.

Is that how you visualize your interactions when you dare to speak with God?

God doesn't merely tolerate your "interruptions" in his daily business. He doesn't resent your requests. He welcomes them. He commands them. In fact, he tips his hand and lets you know that he is preinclined to say yes to you. Here is Jesus' challenge: "Ask and it will be given to you; seek and you will find; knock and the door will be opened to you. For everyone who asks receives; the one who seeks finds; and to the one who knocks, the door will be opened" (Matthew 7:7,8).

You are not an alien or stranger in God's presence anymore. Through your faith in Christ, you are now family. You belong there. Act like you belong there. Be bold when you pray. Claim your blood-bought identity. You are not irritating God with your chutzpah. You are honoring his invitation and promise.

What do you need right now? Ask! Seek! Knock!

Journaling Question

How does it feel knowing you are loved by an incredible God who doesn't want you to be too awestruck to stand in his presence but invites you (encourages you!) to come to him with every little thought and request? How might your prayer life be different if this weren't the case? How should your prayer life be different because it IS the case?

Prayer

Dear Father, thank you for being so accessible. Thank you for loving me as your own dear child and inviting me into your presence so I can talk like family. Help me not forget this amazing invitation in the rush and stress of day-to-day life. Help me be open and communicate more with you! Amen.

PERSISTENT

Jesus told his disciples a parable to show them that they should always pray and not give up. . . . "Will not God bring about justice for his chosen ones, who cry out to him day and night? Will he keep putting them off?"

Luke 18:1,7

Parents don't like it when their children beg and their spouses nag. If you are asked for something and the answer's no, you don't like to hear about it again and again. Wouldn't it be logical to assume, then, that God would be irritated if we ask for something more than once?

Logical? Yes. But in fact, the very opposite is true. He does not see repeated prayers as nagging or begging. "Jesus told his disciples a parable to show them that they should always pray and not give up. . . . 'Will not God bring about justice for his chosen ones, who cry out to him day and night? Will he keep putting them off?'" (Luke 18:1,7).

In Jesus' little story, a widow pestered a judge for justice until he relented. Instead of criticizing the woman for being such a pest, Jesus held her up as a hero and invited all believers to be just like her.

When our first prayer doesn't seem to be granted, we don't know for sure when God is saying no permanently or when his answer is "maybe" or when the answer is "later." What we do know is that the Father not merely tolerates but welcomes and even praises persistent pray-ers. Pray and don't give up!

Journaling Question

Do you have any prayers that you've prayed repeatedly over the years? Do you have any that you've given up on? Maybe it's time to dust them off and keep praying!

2/4/22 –

KK's health – she is very congested and scheduled flu + covid next week –

Prayer

Dear God, thank you for welcoming my repetitive prayers. I know your answer may be something other than what I'm expecting, but you always, *always* answer! And you are always faithful! (Take a moment to pray for anything you may have listed above.) Amen.

FOR OTHERS

Pray also for me, that whenever I speak, words may be given me so that I will fearlessly make known the mystery of the gospel, for which I am an ambassador in chains. Pray that I may declare it fearlessly, as I should.

Ephesians 6:19,20

We all have a selfish streak by nature. When we become aware that we are able to access God's throne through prayer, our first instincts are to care only about ourselves. But just as spiritual growth helps us see the joy and fulfillment that come from serving other people, growth in prayer maturity leads us to think of other people's needs before our own.

St. Paul invited his Asian brothers and sisters to pray for him while a prisoner in Rome, awaiting his trial in imperial court. "Pray also for me, that whenever I speak, words may be given me so that I will fearlessly make known the mystery of the gospel, for which I am an ambassador in chains. Pray that I may declare it fearlessly, as I should" (Ephesians 6:19,20).

The formal word for this kind of praying is *intercession*. I personally have been sustained by the prayers of other wonderful people in stretches of my life when I have been too distracted or lazy to pray for myself. You will not know until you get to heaven how your life has been blessed by the faithful prayers of people who love you.

Could I dare to ask you to pray for me today so that I may proclaim the gospel fearlessly?

Journaling Question

Intercession is powerful! Who are some people who could use your prayers today? Family? Friends? Coworkers? Pastors? Strangers? Make a list, as well as some ideas of what kind of prayers they could use.

- G — dental work + expense
- KK — safety + health
- Kirsten — continue path —
  — to be with you + ask
  you to be in her life / relationship,
- Kevin + Wonnie — discernment as
  they build their foundation
- Bob — find joy, little bits of
  happiness each day, in you, in
  everything

Prayer

Take a moment in prayer for the people you listed above. Praying for others is a powerful thing indeed! Your words will be heard!

TOGETHER

I tell you that if two of you on earth agree about anything they ask for, it will be done for them by my Father in heaven.

Matthew 18:19

Two are better than one. . . . If either of them falls down, one can help the other up.

Ecclesiastes 4:9,10

God loves it when you worship him all by yourself—reading his Word, humming and singing hymn stanzas, and showing thankfulness when you see good things happening. But he likes it as much when you worship him with a group of fellow believers. It shows that you are proud of him, greatly increases your chances of learning things from the wisdom and testimonies of others, and builds up your courage and self-confidence through a living fellowship.

It's the same with your prayer life. God loves to hear from you one-on-one. But he takes such delight in group prayer that he attaches special promises to the experience: "I tell you that if two of you on earth agree about anything they ask for, it will be done for them by my Father in heaven" (Matthew 18:19).

There are many ways to do this: interceding for one another in your worship services, small-group prayer gatherings, online prayer teams, or school groups. The beauty of it is that not only does God show special favor to that kind of praying, but you also end up with deeper friendships as a result. As Solomon wrote in Ecclesiastes 4:9,10, "Two are better than one. . . . If either of them falls down, one can help the other up." Do you have prayer partners?

Journaling Question

Have you ever had a prayer group or prayer partner? If so, what was the experience like? How was it beneficial? If not, do you think it's something that would be useful? Why or why not?

Prayer

Dear Lord, help me remember to pray—not just on my own but also with other believers. Thank you for the gift of fellowship. It strengthens my faith, my friendships, and my connection to you! Amen.

CONFIDENT

**When you ask, you must believe and not doubt,
because the one who doubts is like a wave of the sea,
blown and tossed by the wind. That person should not
expect to receive anything from the Lord. Such a person
is double-minded and unstable in all they do.**

James 1:6-8

Here's another prayer misconception that God would like to correct. You would think that an appropriate attitude for needy, often foolish, often backsliding Christians when they approach the throne would be abject humility. You would think that we would offer up our requests timidly. You would think that we would tiptoe around him, walking on eggshells of fear, murmuring our needs quickly, and then backing away toward the door.

Nonsense, says the apostle James. You are God's beloved child, a royal prince or princess of heaven, a royal priest of the heavenly temple. God wants you to believe him when he says he eagerly receives information about the parts of your life in which you need help. "When you ask, you must believe and not doubt, because the one who doubts is like a wave of the sea, blown and tossed by the wind. That person should not expect to receive anything from the Lord. Such a person is double-minded and unstable in all they do" (James 1:6-8).

Doubt comes from Satan. If he can plant doubts in your brain and lead you to suspect that God is laughing at you, has contempt for you, is ignoring you, or is blowing off your troubles, your prayer voice will be timid indeed and soon stop. But believe his Word! Claim your new identity! Speak up! No fear! No doubts! He smiles when he sees you approach.

Journaling Question

What is your attitude like when you pray? Do you tend to be timid and quiet? Or are you loud and bold? Write a confident prayer to Jesus, being certain of your identity in Christ. No fear! No doubts! Speak up!

Prayer

Take some time to pray earnestly the prayer you wrote above.

IN JESUS' NAME

**My Father will give you whatever you ask in my name.
Until now you have not asked for anything in my name.
Ask and you will receive, and your joy will be complete.**

John 16:23,24

Just before he was arrested, tortured, and murdered, Jesus spent some intense hours with his disciples. He gave them important information about carrying on with their lives and ministry when they would no longer have his physical presence in their midst.

He especially wanted them to know that their close relationship with the Father would continue because their Savior would still be their personal link to his throne. "My Father will give you whatever you ask *in my name*. Until now you have not asked for anything *in my name*. Ask and you will receive, and your joy will be complete" (John 16:23,24).

When you listen to Christians pray, you will often hear them end their prayers with "in Jesus' name." Mentioning the proper name of Christ is a sweet custom. But that's not all Jesus meant—just to attach his name to your heavenly communications.

Praying in Jesus' name means believing that he is your Savior, that you are now considered God's child, and all this is only because of Jesus.

It also means that you pray according to his name in the sense of his self-revelation, that is, that you are following his charge to put God's agenda first.

Journaling Question

When you do something in someone's name, you're assuming their identity. What does it mean to you that Jesus says you can pray in his name? What does this say about your relationship with God and how he views your prayers?

Prayer

Dear heavenly Father, I'm so humble and grateful that I can approach you because of what your Son did for me on the cross. Please help me focus on YOUR agenda for my life. In Jesus' name I pray. Amen.

GOD'S PROMISES TO THOSE WHO PRAY

Pastor Mark Jeske

I AM WITH YOU

Never will I leave you; never will I forsake you.

Hebrews 13:5

Of all the losses that the human race sustained when Adam and Eve were driven out of the Garden of Eden, one of the most grievous was the loss of direct and immediate contact with God. Now that relationship would have to be built and nourished "at a distance," as it were. Because our minds are clouded with sin and weakness, we tend not to believe in things we can't see or touch. We are all doubting Thomases at times.

Sometimes God may seem very remote or not there at all. Pink Floyd has a line in one of their songs, "Is there anybody out there?" In your darker moments of weakness and despair, have you ever feared that nobody was listening to your cries for help?

God no longer physically walks the earth as he did in the person of Jesus Christ, but he is always present in many ways. "Never will I leave you; never will I forsake you" (Hebrews 13:5). His Spirit fills the universe. His Word reveals his mind and purpose and mighty acts. The splash of baptismal water is your adoption ceremony and the seal of his ownership claims. The Lord's Supper merges his divine body and blood with yours.

He is near to you right now.

Journaling Question

Describe a time in your life when you felt far away from God. Often, during those challenging times, God is closer than you could imagine. Looking back on that time in your life, can you now see this to be true? How so?

Prayer

Dear God, I know you will never leave me. Even though I can't see you physically, face-to-face, you have promised to walk with me through this life. It's often hard to remember that during the tough times. Please help me be aware of your constant presence through all the ups and downs of my life. Amen.

I SEE AND HEAR AND ACT

When you pray, go into your room, close the door and pray to your Father, who is unseen. Then your Father, who sees what is done in secret, will reward you.

Matthew 6:6

It was my privilege to teach in a high school for two years. How different the classroom looks from the front! When I was a student, slouching down low in the back seat in the corner, I thought the teacher wouldn't be able to see me dozing, doodling, or doing other homework. Ha! You can see everything from the front.

Sinful mortals sometimes assume that God must not be tracking what's going on on the surface of planet Earth. Perhaps they fear that the wicked are getting away with murder. Perhaps they fear that their own needs go unnoticed by a distant deity.

Au contraire. "When you pray, go into your room, close the door and pray to your Father, who is unseen. Then your Father, who sees what is done in secret, will reward you" (Matthew 6:6). God's ability to monitor details of earthly life is staggering. The Bible says that he has counted every hair on your head and that no sparrow can fall from the sky without God being aware of it and granting permission.

Wherever you live, wherever you go, no matter the trouble, your God can see what's happening in your life. Whether you speak, sing, whisper, or think your prayers, your God can hear them all. Messages sent—messages received. Always.

Journaling Question

How does it make you feel to know that not even a sparrow drops from the sky without God noticing it? If God cares that much about a creature he *didn't* die for, what does that mean for how much he cares about you . . . someone he *did* die for?

Prayer

Dear God, thank you for always noticing what's going on in my life. I know nothing surprises you, nothing gets by you; you see it all. Help me live confidently in the knowledge that you care about every little detail of my life. Amen.

I CARE

Cast all your anxiety on him because he cares for you.

1 Peter 5:7

I. Love. You.

We are all starving to hear those three words. They are consumable. We burn them up to keep going in a hostile and cruel world, to keep going when our own self-doubts and self-hatred gnaw at our self-confidence. We can never hear those words enough.

How could you want to pray to a God who didn't love you? You might bargain with such a god or try to pay him off or earn some points with rituals, but you couldn't bare your soul.

The One who invites your prayers made himself low for you. He emptied himself, taking the very nature of a servant. He was born in a barn, lived simply, taught the Word, bore scorn, was arrested and unjustly convicted, and endured the scourge and the cross in order to break the power of sin's curse over you. On the third day, he triumphantly rose from death and promises a similar resurrection to all who trust and believe in him.

Why did he do all those things? Because he loves you. And so you can "cast all your anxiety on him because he cares for you" (1 Peter 5:7).

Journaling Question

How does having a God who loves you enough to die for you make a difference in how you go through life? What does it mean to you? How does it make life easier? How does it make tough times more bearable?

_____

_____

_____

_____

_____

_____

_____

_____

_____

_____

_____

Prayer

Dear God, thank you for loving me. I know I haven't done anything to earn that love—yet you still sent your Son all the way to the cross to show your love to me. Help me remember this when I pray. Amen.

I ACT BECAUSE YOU ASKED

**"Because the poor are plundered and the needy groan,
I will now arise," says the Lord**

Psalm 12:5

Have you ever watched children with a piñata at a birthday party? A hollow animal has been constructed of thin plaster. The blindfolded children swing a stick until someone hits the animal. As it breaks, a shower of candy and gifts pours out. When you pray, you may feel blindfolded and feel as though you are flailing about in the dark. But a prayer to God's throne in the name of Jesus always connects with a heavenly piñata, and blessings rain down *because you were swinging your stick*!

C. S. Lewis calls this the dignity of causality. God gives you and me the honor of influencing what happens tomorrow. The reason? When God hears the prayers of his children, he not only cares; he acts. "'Because the poor are plundered and the needy groan, I will now arise,' says the Lord" (Psalm 12:5). Did you catch that? God loves you enough to let your thoughts and ideas and needs lead him to change his governance of the world.

Your prayers make a difference. Every prayer you say changes something somewhere. The future is not hardened and unmovable. Your prayers can alter the future.

Journaling Question

Your prayers *actually change things*. How does this make you feel about the importance of prayer? Does it make you want to spend more time in prayer? Why?

Prayer

Dear God, I know you not only hear my prayers, but you ACT on my prayers. Help me not take prayer for granted and remember that my prayers make a difference. Amen.

WE'VE ALREADY WON

**In this world you will have trouble. But take heart!
I have overcome the world.**

John 16:33

I can't blame you if you have concluded that the world is going to hell and Satan won after all. Any cop could tell you that most days things look pretty bleak. The human race is not evolving into better people. The last century was the bloodiest in history. Increases in technology only mean that people can rob and kill on a bigger scale.

People who feel defeated probably don't feel like praying much. What's the use? Everything's going downhill. I'm doomed. Nothing is working for me. When gloomy thoughts like that overtake your mind, recall Jesus' words: "In this world you will have trouble. But take heart! I have overcome the world" (John 16:33).

The American/Philippine retreat and defeat at Bataan and Corregidor during World War II was a miserable time for the Allies, but it would have been much more bearable if they could have seen just three years into the future—the Japanese surrender on the battleship *Missouri* in Tokyo Bay.

Jesus' prophecy came true. His disciples did indeed have trouble—persecution, imprisonment, death. But their faith in Jesus' ultimate victory sustained them. Now they wear a crown of glory, and you will too. Take heart!

Journaling Question

Take a moment to make a list of some of the things you worry about in your life and in the world today. When you're done, write in large letters at the very top: GOD'S WON THE BATTLE! You don't have to worry about ANY of the woes of the world!

Prayer

Dear Lord, sometimes I get anxious about (fill in the blank by glancing at your list above). Help me remember I don't need to worry about the things of this world. You've got it all under control. And I can take confidence in the fact that you've won the biggest battle—against Satan and death. Amen.

GOD AND MY NEEDS

"Because he loves me," says the Lord, "I will rescue him; I will protect him, for he acknowledges my name. He will call upon me, and I will answer him; I will be with him in trouble, I will deliver him and honor him."

Psalm 91:14,15

What are you afraid of?

When men hear a question like that, they go into John Wayne mode: "I ain't afraid o' nuthin', ma'am." Well, baloney. We all have fears, whether we admit it or not. Men are afraid of being seen as weak. They fear losing respect, losing their jobs, losing their place. Women fear for their personal safety and the safety of those they love. Women fear for their family's health and wellness. Children have a thousand fears, of which the terror of abandonment is near the top.

All of us fear death and the dying process. And I think if we're honest, we would admit to being vulnerable to Satan's whisperings that our faith is a fraud and that there is no God and no help as we struggle to survive.

Here is God's solemn promise to you: "'Because he loves me,' says the Lord, 'I will rescue him; I will protect him, for he acknowledges my name. He will call upon me, and I will answer him; I will be with him in trouble, I will deliver him and honor him'" (Psalm 91:14,15).

God sees you. He cares about you. He knows what you need and when. He acts, always right on time.

Journaling Question

What are some of your biggest fears? How does it feel to know God is more powerful than all of them?

Prayer

Dear God, thank you for being bigger than all my wildest fears. Thank you for seeing me and knowing my needs. Help me continue to call on your name when I'm feeling afraid. Amen.

THE HOLY SPIRIT

The Spirit helps us in our weakness. We do not know what we ought to pray for, but the Spirit himself intercedes for us through wordless groans.

Romans 8:26

The Holy Spirit is a prayer hero. Yes—there is actually a lot of praying that goes on within the Holy Trinity itself. Seriously!

You recall, of course, how often Jesus prayed to his heavenly Father during his time on earth. Now at the Father's right hand, Jesus pleads for the believers on the basis of his saving work. Did you know that the Spirit is a terrific pray-er also? "The Spirit helps us in our weakness. We do not know what we ought to pray for, but the Spirit himself intercedes for us through wordless groans" (Romans 8:26).

Aspiring writers who desire their work to be published should realize that they need an editor. Editors clean up early drafts so that the final copy says just what the author needs it to say. Isn't it a spectacular comfort to know that our sometimes incoherent, sometimes stammered, sometimes selfish, sometimes misdirected prayers go to the Father, not only through the name of Jesus but also through the editorial desk of God the Holy Spirit? Amazing!

This means that you can feel free to pray even when you fear your thoughts aren't completely collected or when you're having trouble putting your feelings into words. The Holy Spirit will bring perfect prayers to the Father. Every time.

Journaling Question

Sometimes we're afraid to speak because we're afraid of sounding stupid or of not having the right words. Jot down a time when this may have happened to you. How did it make you feel? How does it feel knowing that even if you don't have the words to pray, the Spirit will help decipher your mutterings into the perfect prayer before God?

Prayer

Dear God, thank you for sending your Spirit to help present my prayers before you. Sometimes I feel tongued-tied, like I don't have the right words, or that I'm always repeating the same prayer words over and over until they become meaning- less. Help me rely on your Spirit and try to give voice to the thoughts I'm thinking. Amen.

ABOUT THE WRITERS

Pastor Mike Novotny has served God's people in full-time ministry since 2007 in Madison and, most recently, at The CORE in Appleton, Wisconsin. He also serves as the lead speaker for Time of Grace, where he shares the good news about Jesus through television, print, and online platforms. Mike loves seeing people grasp the depth of God's amazing grace and unstoppable mercy. His wife continues to love him (despite plenty of reasons not to), and his two daughters open his eyes to the love of God for every Christian. When not talking about Jesus or dating his wife/girls, Mike loves playing soccer, running, and reading.

Pastor Mark Jeske brought the good news of Jesus Christ to viewers of *Time of Grace* for 18 years. He is currently the senior pastor at St. Marcus Church, a thriving multicultural congregation in Milwaukee, Wisconsin. Mark is the author of several books and dozens of devotional booklets on various topics. He and his wife, Carol, have four adult children.

ABOUT TIME OF GRACE

Time of Grace is an independent, donor-funded ministry that connects people to God's grace—his love, glory, and power—so they realize the temporary things of life don't satisfy. What brings satisfaction is knowing that because Jesus lived, died, and rose for all of us, we have access to the eternal God—right now and forever.

To discover more, please visit timeofgrace.org or call 800.661.3311.

HELP SHARE GOD'S MESSAGE OF GRACE!

Every gift you give helps Time of Grace reach people around the world with the good news of Jesus. Your generosity and prayer support take the gospel of grace to others through our ministry outreach and help them experience a satisfied life as they see God all around them.

Give today at timeofgrace.org/give or by calling 800.661.3311.

Thank you!